CHURCH MATTERS!

CHURCH MATTERS!

Andrew Anderson

Bible Churches
growing together

CROSSWAY BOOKS

ISBN 1 85684 026 3

Typeset by Medcalf Type Ltd, Bicester, Oxon
Printed in Great Britain for Crossway Books, Kingfisher House,
7 High Green, Great Shelford, Cambridge by
Cox & Wyman Ltd, Cardiff Road, Reading

Contents

Preface

Churches come in all shapes and sizes.

- There are Anglican churches, Presbyterian churches, Baptist churches, Pentecostal churches, United Reformed . . . and so on.

- There are large churches with crowded congregations; there are medium-sized churches; there are small churches which sometimes struggle to keep going.

- There are churches whose services are predictable; others totally unpredictable. Some sing only psalms, some only hymns, some only spiritual songs; while others mix the ingredients: a bit of this and a bit of that.

- There are churches with a minister and churches without a minister; churches with elders and churches without elders; churches that baptise believers and churches that baptise babies.

- There are churches where tongues and prophecies and healings are practised and churches where they are not.

Yes, churches do come in all shapes and sizes.

When you take account of all the differences of size, denomination, style, ministry and gift, the permutations are enough to make your head swim. How does anyone choose which church to join? A new Christian faced with such variety could feel like a child gazing at a sweet counter. Take your pick!

There is, however, a much more basic point of difference. Churches vary in what they actually believe and preach. What a church stands for and what its message is, is after all fundamental.

Some churches are liberal in their theology. They dismiss bits of the Bible, deny some of the basic truths of the Christian faith and seem to major on the social and minimise the spiritual.

Other churches have a strong ritualistic emphasis. While they may maintain the need for personal salvation, they teach that salvation comes through the sacraments of the church and is to some extent merited by the deeds or the devotion of the individual.

Evangelical churches stand in contrast to churches that are liberal or ritualistic. They believe the Bible and seek to proclaim the Bible message: the good news of salvation for sinners by God's grace alone, received through faith in Christ alone.

So choosing a church is not just a matter of personal preference, it is a matter of principle. A true Christian will want to be a member of a trustworthy church: an evangelical church.

There are evangelical churches within the major denominations. But some evangelical churches are independent of denominational structures. The aim of this booklet is simply to set out the biblical principles for which independent evangelical churches stand.

I am most grateful to my fellow-members of the Theological Committee of the Fellowship of Independent

Evangelical Churches: Paul Brown, Brian Edwards, David Middleton, Colin Smith and Jonathan Stephen for their stimulus, counsel and sheer good friendship, and to Derek Prime for giving a push-start to our thinking on the inter-relatedness of New Testament independent churches.

Andrew Anderson

Chapter 1

What is an Evangelical?

She was run off her feet. None of the others was free to admit him to the ward when the porter wheeled him up from Casualty.

'Name? . . . Date of birth? . . . Religion?' quizzed the nurse. 'Independent evangelical,' replied the patient, wincing with pain.

'Independent what?!' The usual answer was C of E, occasionally Methodist or Salvation Army. But what on earth was an independent evangelical? And how did you spell it? Her ball-point got hopelessly stuck at 'evan . . .', and she was glad to get back to the drug round.

What is an independent evangelical church? The flustered nurse was not the first to wonder. It is understandable that many people don't know what it means; most churches are part of a large denomination with a name almost as familiar as Kellogg's. 'Independent evangelical' is hardly a household name!

As a matter of fact there are hundreds of independent evangelical churches in the United Kingdom. Many of them are quite small, but some of the largest congregations in the country are independent evangelical. They stand outside any denominational structure and they stand for the historic evangelical gospel. To explain what independent evangelical churches are we must start with the word 'evangelical'.

What is an evangelical? The way some people talk you would think that evangelicals were one of the latest religious sects to spring from sunny California. The name seems to conjure up in the mind a bunch of arm-waving fanatics, or televangelists whose business practices and private lives have hardly been a good advertisement for any brand of religion. Certainly, if the portrayal of evangelicals by the media were accurate we would be wiser to keep quiet about the name. The fact is, however, that true evangelicals are not ashamed of the word.

Not that it is always used accurately. 'Evangelical' is often confused with 'evangelistic'; people use one word when they mean the other. The two are, of course, related; they both begin with '*evangel*' and that Greek word means 'good news'. 'Evangelistic' describes the activity of spreading the good news of Jesus Christ: a church is evangelistic if it is making an effort to bring people to a personal faith in Christ; a book or a service or a sermon is evangelistic if it presents the gospel in a direct way. Evangelicals ought always to be evangelistic, but 'evangelistic' means the sharing of belief and 'evangelical' describes the belief itself.

'Evangelical' refers to a doctrinal position, a system of belief. The word has an honoured history and was in use even before the Reformation in the sixteenth century. It signifies belief in the Bible and belief in the gospel as the Bible declares it.

Evangelicals have deep convictions about the Bible: for them the Bible is God's word written. Though over forty human authors wrote its books, it has a divine Author; it is God-breathed. Though completed nearly 2,000 years ago, it needs no correction or supplement for God has given his final revelation in his word. What he spoke, he still speaks. Evangelicals accept the entire

Bible as the word of God and they accept its authority on all matters of faith and practice. It is because evangelicals view the Bible in this way that they believe the gospel as God has revealed it in the Bible. They believe that God saves sinners on the basis of the atoning sacrifice that his Son offered for them when he died on the cross. They do not tamper with this gospel either by adding to what God has said, or by taking away from it.

Evangelicals are happy to state what they believe. Though they accept that true religion is a matter of the heart, they do not go along with the idea that because this is so its substance cannot be put into words! Indeed, finding truth stated in Scripture, they see it as their duty to believe the truth, to obey the truth, to preach and teach the truth and when necessary to defend the truth. So evangelical churches and evangelical movements usually publish a statement of faith setting out exactly what they believe. A good example is the *What We Believe* statement published by the Fellowship of Independent Evangelical Churches, a grouping of over 400 local churches.

When the FIEC was formed in 1922, its founders set out a statement of the essentials of the evangelical faith that highlighted the great doctrines of historic, biblical Christianity and deliberately avoided matters over which there are differences of interpretation. In 1991 a gathering of representatives of affiliated churches agreed to a reworded statement which expresses the same great truths in a more contemporary way. It is a statement that all true evangelicals, whatever their church affiliation, would agree with.

What We Believe

1. GOD

There is one God, who exists eternally in three distinct but equal persons: the Father, the Son, and the Holy Spirit. God is unchangeable in his holiness, justice, wisdom and love. He is the almighty Creator, Saviour and Judge who sustains and governs all things according to his sovereign will for his own glory.

2. THE BIBLE

God has revealed himself in the Bible, which consists of the Old and New Testaments alone. Every word was inspired by God through human authors, so that the Bible as originally given is in its entirety the word of God, without error and fully reliable in fact and doctrine. The Bible alone speaks with final authority and is always sufficient for all matters of belief and practice.

3. THE HUMAN RACE

All men and women, being created in the image of God, have inherent and equal dignity and worth. Their greatest purpose is to obey, worship and love God. As a result of the fall of our first parents, every aspect of human nature has been corrupted and all men and women are without spiritual life, guilty sinners and hostile to God. Every person is therefore under the just condemnation of God and needs to be born again, forgiven and reconciled to God in order to know and please him.

4. THE LORD JESUS CHRIST

The Lord Jesus Christ is fully God and fully man. He was conceived by the Holy Spirit, born of a virgin, and lived a sinless life in obedience to the Father. He taught with authority and all his words are true. On the cross he died in the place of sinners, bearing God's punishment for their sin, redeeming them by his blood. He rose from the dead and in his resurrection body ascended into heaven where he is exalted as Lord of all. He intercedes for his people in the presence of the Father.

5. SALVATION

Salvation is entirely a work of God's grace and cannot be earned or deserved. It has been accomplished by the Lord Jesus Christ and is offered to all in the gospel. God in his love forgives sinners whom he calls, granting them repentance and faith. All who believe in Christ are justified by faith alone, adopted into the family of God and receive eternal life.

6. THE HOLY SPIRIT

The Holy Spirit has been sent from heaven to glorify Christ and to apply his work of salvation. He convicts sinners, imparts spiritual life and gives a true understanding of the Scriptures. He indwells all believers, brings assurance of salvation and produces increasing likeness to Christ. He builds up the Church and empowers its members for worship, service and mission.

7. THE CHURCH

The universal church is the body of which Christ is the head and to which all who are saved belong. It is made visible in local churches, which are congregations of believers who are committed to each other for the worship of God, the preaching of the word, the administering of baptism and the Lord's Supper, for pastoral care and discipline, and for evangelism. The unity of the body of Christ is expressed within and between churches by mutual love, care and encouragement. True fellowship between churches exists only where they are faithful to the gospel.

8. BAPTISM AND THE LORD'S SUPPER

Baptism and the Lord's Supper have been given to the churches by Christ as visible signs of the gospel. Baptism is a symbol of union with Christ and entry into his church but does not impart spiritual life. The Lord's Supper is a commemoration of Christ's sacrifice offered once for all and involves no change in the bread and wine. All its blessings are received by faith.

9. THE FUTURE

The Lord Jesus Christ will return in glory. He will raise the dead and judge the world in righteousness. The wicked will be sent to eternal punishment and the righteous will be welcomed into a life of eternal joy in fellowship with God. God will make all things new and will be glorified for ever.

These are great truths: they are humbling, saving, glorious truths. They should move us to praise God.

The evangelical faith must never be thought of as one aspect of the Christian faith; one emphasis that can sit comfortably alongside other views. It is the original and authentic Christian faith; it is the gospel. Evangelical churches preach the only gospel there is: the good news of salvation in Christ.

We've looked at what evangelical means; now it's time for us to look at the church.

Chapter 2
Church Matters!

Many Christians are enthusiastic about their church; it has a major place in their lives. But, strange to say, that is not true of all Christians. Some church members seem to be more interested in Christian activities and events that happen outside their own church's life than those that happen within it. Stranger still, some people who claim to be Christian and think of themselves as being keen Christians sit loose to membership of the local church and do not join at all.

Is the church important? Does church matter?

The answer has to be a resounding 'yes' and for one simple reason: the church matters to God. There can be no doubt about that, for time and again the Bible shows us that God gives the church a very high priority.

Before Christ came into the world, God had his chosen people and true believers in Israel delighted to gather together. When Christ came, he declared as his great purpose, 'I will build my church' (Mt 16:18). When he returned to heaven, the apostles continued his work. The Book of Acts is not just the story of the evangelising of thousands of individuals; it is the record of the planting and the nurturing of churches. Most of the letters in the New Testament were written to local churches. Those that were not are all concerned with pastoral matters that affect the life of churches. The Revelation, the climax of the Bible, was given to assure the church under the pressure of persecution that Christ the king and head of the church knew all that was going on and had the church in his powerful hand.

The church certainly matters to God, so it surely should matter to every Christian. It is true that God is the God of the individual and that each believer is personally saved by Christ, yet Christians are never thought of simply as individuals. The Bible always views the life of the Christian in the context of the local church. Indeed, no believer is thought of as being other than a living part of Christ's church.

Evangelicals have rightly stressed the necessity of knowing Jesus Christ as personal Lord and Saviour, and the joy of it, too. That is an evangelical distinctive and entirely biblical, but such an emphasis should never be to the exclusion of the corporate aspect of salvation. Neglect of the church can never be justified: we are not saved to live in splendid isolation; we are saved to be together.

The church matters, but

WHAT IS THE CHURCH?
This question must be asked, for in all the talk about the church at the present time there is amazing confusion as to what the church really is.

Some think of the church in terms of buildings
The word is often used for the place where Christians meet, but in the Bible the church is not a building, it is people. Though the Scriptures say so much on the subject of the church, they do not once use the word in the sense of a building. Of course neither our Lord nor his apostles had special buildings of their own in which

to meet and the believers in New Testament times met in the open air, in one another's homes or, if necessary, in a large room. They met wherever they could; it did not matter to them where, because church to them was not a place, it was people.

Some think of the church in terms of officials
They have been taught that bishops are in the succession of the apostles and that 'where the bishop is, there the church is'. But it is impossible to prove apostolic succession through an unbroken line of men, and it is quite unnecessary to do so. The true apostolic ministry today is to be found wherever the apostles' doctrine, the apostolic gospel, is preached. The church is never defined in terms of officials.

Others think of the church in terms of sacraments
They believe that people are made Christians in their baptism and that they are sustained in the Christian life after that by their participation in the eucharist. Regeneration comes through baptism; grace is conveyed through the channel of the sacraments. Such a view is contrary to what the Scriptures teach about salvation, and about the sacraments too.

Still others think of the church in terms of territory
Many claim that if you were born in England you have the right to belong to the established church of the land, to be christened, to be married in church and to be buried by one of its ministers. Some of those who attend regularly, and are more involved, do so because they like that sort of thing!

The degree of confusion demands that we have a biblical answer to the question 'What is the church?'.

The church is the covenant people of God. The Bible tells us that God has chosen to enter into relationship with certain people – a relationship so special that they are his people and he is their God (Ex 6:7; Heb 8:8–12). In the Old Testament that covenant relationship was with Israel who were chosen simply because of his love and grace. Now, the people of God are all those who know Jesus Christ, the Saviour who laid down his life for them (Jn 10:14–15).

The Greek word for church is *ecclesia*; our English word 'ecclesiastic' comes straight from it. It originally meant 'called out'. When an emergency arose in one of their cities, the Greeks would call out a body of citizens to come together to decide what should be done. They were called out to come together for a purpose. The word came to mean 'assembly' and, though the original meaning 'called out' may have been lost by the time the New Testament was written, it is a very appropriate word to describe a gathering of Christians.

The church is a company of people who have been called out from everyone else and been gathered together for the special purpose of glorifying God.

Think of those early days of the church. An apostle would come to a pagan city with all its open evil, as Paul for instance came to Corinth or to Thessalonica. He would preach the gospel and, through his message, God would call people out. They were forgiven, cleansed from the guilt of all their sins and made new people in Christ. They were called out from their old ways, their pagan worship and their immoral living and they were gathered together as a group of Christians to be the church in their city. They still lived in the city, but they belonged to the church: they were in the world but they were not like the world any more.

Called out and called together: that is a good

description of what the church is in its very essence. The church Paul founded in Corinth was 'the church of God in Corinth . . . those sanctified in Christ Jesus and called to be holy' (1 Cor 1:2). The string of scattered churches that Peter writes to were 'God's elect . . . chosen according to the foreknowledge of God the Father, by the sanctifying work of the Spirit, for obedience to Jesus Christ and sprinkling by his blood'. They were so special that they were described as 'a chosen people, a royal priesthood, a holy nation, a people belonging to God . . . called . . . out of darkness into his wonderful light' (1 Pet 1:1–2; 2:9).

The church is no ordinary society, nor is membership of it open simply to anyone who takes the notion. It is the covenant people of God and each one is called. The call of God makes the church of God.

A CHURCH AND THE CHURCH

The word 'church' is used in the New Testament over ninety times. Usually it refers to a gathering of believers in a particular locality, but in a dozen places it refers to something much bigger than the local church. When Paul says to the Ephesians that God has appointed Christ to be 'head over everything for the church' or to the Colossians that Christ is the 'head of the body, the church', he is not merely thinking of their local churches in Ephesus or Colossae (Eph 1:22; Col 1:18). He has something much bigger than a particular local church in mind when he movingly declares: 'Christ loved the church and gave himself up for her to make her holy, cleansing her by the washing with water through the word, and to present her to himself as a radiant church, without stain or wrinkle or any other blemish, but holy and blameless' (Eph 5:25–27).

You see 'church' is used at two distinct levels. It

sometimes means a company of Christians in one place: *a local church*. It sometimes means all the Christians everywhere who have ever been or will be; believers worldwide from every age, past, present and future: *the universal church*. The former is an expression of the latter, for however it is viewed, the church is always made up of those called out, and Christ is always its head.

Ultimately, of course, only God knows who belongs to the church. It is possible for people to be accepted as members of a local church without being truly Christian; not truly members of the universal church. And occasionally a true Christian, a member of that great universal church, may be found in some isolated and spiritually barren place where there is no local church to join.

CHURCH AND GOSPEL

It will be obvious that our thinking about the church is bound to be controlled by our understanding of the gospel. That is implied in all we have said about the church, but it is so important that we must spell it out in a little more detail.

It is quite a common idea, even among evangelical people, that the main teaching in the Bible is the gospel of personal salvation, and that teaching on the church is a separate issue and a matter of secondary importance: an optional extra like sports wheels on a car – nice to have but not essential. People who take the Bible very seriously on its doctrine of salvation sometimes sit quite loose to it when it comes to the doctrine of the church. Of course they believe that the church must preach the gospel, but in their thinking they actually separate church from gospel. They may think that the Bible has little to say on the subject; that what it says is not definitive, and that, therefore, we are left to organise the church pretty well any way we like.

Such thinking is unbiblical. Just consider again for a moment the Bible's message of good news. We must never get away from it – it is basic to everything. The Bible says that though we were made by God, we are all rebels against him. Our sins are a barrier that has come between us and God; we need to be reconciled to him. They stain our souls and we need to be cleansed. Spiritually dead and totally incapable of remedying the situation, we need that radical spiritual transformation, the new birth, that only the Spirit of God can bring about. Our spiritual condition now will have eternal consequences, for until it is remedied we are travelling the broad road to destruction. This is bad news, the situation is black indeed, and the gospel is light shining in such darkness.

The good news tells us that Christ Jesus came into the world to save sinners. Out of love that none of us deserves, God sent his Son into this rebellious world. He became a man, one with us. He died on the cross to save his people from their sins and with his precious blood he redeemed them. All who repent and trust him are freely forgiven their sins, cleansed from their guilt, made right with God and brought into that family where God is their Father and all other believers their brothers and sisters.

So the gospel and the church are not separate. The gospel actually *creates* the church, for it is the good news that brings the church into being. And the gospel *defines* the church. It says exactly what it is. It says who are God's people and who are not. The church is made up of those who, through the gospel, have a personal experience of Jesus Christ as their Saviour and Lord. That is true of the one universal church and that should be true of the many local churches.

Church and gospel are inseparably linked. To separate

them is both unbiblical and dangerous. If the church is not seen in terms of the gospel, people who have no true saving knowledge of Christ will be admitted to the membership of the Church. And the effect of that is that the church actually contradicts the gospel, for it confuses those who are God's people with those who are not.

To sum up, the church matters to God and should matter to us. The church, whether universal or local, is a company of called-out people, the covenant people of God. The church and the gospel are inseparably linked, for the gospel creates the church and the gospel defines who is a member of the universal church of Jesus Christ and who may join a local church.

But how should local churches be organised?

Chapter 3

Why Independent?

Independent churches are churches that govern their own affairs entirely. It is the local church that appoints its own officers and calls its own minister. Each church receives and cares for its own members. Each raises its own finances and administers its own funds. Independent churches are autonomous. That means they are self-governing in the sense that they are not directed or controlled by or accountable to any denomination or group outside the local church.

An arrangement like this might seem strange to those who are used to thinking of the local church as being, in some measure at least, under the authority of a centrally governed denomination. Most denominations have central offices and central funds. Church buildings are often owned by the denomination, and ministers are approved and appointed by a central body. There are officials who have authority over a grouping of churches in a region (some nationally, some even internationally) and these officials exercise considerable influence over what each local congregation may or may not do. Of course the structures differ: some are episcopal, some presbyterian and so on.

Is it right for churches to be independent or should they come under some connexional authority?

If the issue were to be decided by majority vote, the connexionalists would have it by a long chalk. The majority of churches in the United Kingdom come within some type of connexional structure. But such issues are not to be decided merely by numbers. The deciding factor for evangelical Christians must always be this: what does Scripture teach?

Some maintain that the New Testament does not have much to say on the matter of church government. They claim that what it does say simply describes the unstructured life of the church in its early days before there had been time to develop a permanent structure. So, they argue, we are free to develop whatever system of church government and church relationships we feel best. The case of independency versus connexionalism is to be decided on the purely pragmatic grounds of what has proved to be the most satisfactory in history and experience.

But is it true that the New Testament says so little on this important matter? Indeed, if Scripture is our authoritative guide in all matters of belief and practice, surely we may expect it to give us sufficient guidance on such a vital issue as where the authority over the local church does rest. We must look again at Scripture and see what it says. And if we find a lack of central organisation, we must avoid the danger of judging that by our ideas of order and efficiency and of trying to improve on it by imposing on the churches a form that God may never have intended.

So let's look at the New Testament and see how the local churches were governed and how they related.

The first thing that stands out, as we focus on the young churches in action in the New Testament, is that they lived and ordered their affairs under the lordship of Jesus Christ. He had bought the church with his blood and he was acknowledged as the head of the church. He directed the churches by his word and by his Spirit.

Christ is the head of the church and he has every right to rule. That stands out clearly in the New Testament and that is something about which all who profess to be Christians agree. The question is this: '*how* does Christ rule?' Does he rule directly over each church, or does he rule (at least partly) through some central body and its officials?

The last book of the Bible gives an insight into just that issue. There were seven churches, one in each of the seven key towns in the province of Asia Minor. Christ knows them individually, cares for them individually and, through John, writes to each a separate letter. It is true that all who have ears to hear are commanded to hear what the Spirit says to the churches because in what Christ says to each there are lessons to be learned by all. But he deals with them one by one. The spiritual life of some of those churches was ebbing very low. Some were harbouring teachers of error. But Christ warns of his own personal intervention in judgement if they will not put their own house in order. He does not refer the matter to any body outside the local church which can exercise authority over the churches, nor does he give the group of churches authority over the individual churches within it. Christ ruled each church directly. That is true of all the New Testament churches.

The New Testament churches did not act as if they were accountable to an outside body, nor did they look to such a body to make decisions for them. Rather, under Christ their head, they appear to have acted freely and spontaneously. They were self-governing and independent of outside control, though never independent of Christ. This can be demonstrated in a number of ways each of which concerns major issues at the very heart of church life.

The local church appointed its own officers (Acts 6:1–6; 14:23; 1 Tim 3:1–13; Tit 1:5–9). In the case of the seven selected men in Acts 6, the apostles told the Jerusalem church to make its own choice. It is true that in the case of elders Paul and his helpers were involved in the earliest appointments, but it was natural that church planters should have been involved in the selection of the first church leaders. However, once the churches were established with an initial leadership, the apostle Paul simply stated what graces and gifts are required of an elder and a deacon and left it to the church to make its own appointments without any need of approval from outside. The appointment of those who would lead the church, teach the word and care for the flock was a big responsibility, but it was entrusted to each local church.

The local church disciplined its own members (Mt 18:15–17; 1 Cor 5:4–5). Both Christ and Paul gave clear instructions on the matter of discipline, and both laid the responsibility for the exercise of it on the shoulders of the local church. Take for example our Lord's teaching. If a believer was sinned against by a Christian brother, he was to take certain steps, in sequence. In the first place he was to see the brother privately. If that failed, he was to face him with his fault in the presence of two or three others. If that failed, the offended person was to tell it to the church. And if the offender refused to listen to the church, the church was to discipline him and to treat the unrepentant offender as if he were not a member of the Christian family at all, but a heathen man. It was the local church that had to take action.

Of course such discipline is exceptional and is to be exercised in the context of a loving church that cares for each of its members. But it is the local church that is reckoned to be competent to deal with matters of church discipline, and there is no court of appeal higher than the local church.

The local church ordered its own worship (1 Cor 11:17ff; 14:26ff). This too was a great responsibility, because the worship of the true and living God must never be treated lightly. The apostles had to warn the churches of pitfalls to avoid and they exhorted them that 'everything should be done in a fitting and orderly way'. Yet the conduct of worship, as also the administration of baptism and the observance of the Lord's Supper, was left in the hands of the local churches and their leaders.

The local church commissioned its own missionaries (Acts 13:1-3). The gospel must be preached to all nations and new churches must be planted and nurtured. The local churches had a vital part to play in this. It was they who commissioned workers and sent them to the work for which the Holy Spirit had called them.

The local church appointed its own officers, disciplined its own members, ordered its own worship and commissioned its own workers. Through these particulars a general principle emerges: the local church was considered competent, under Christ, to order all its own affairs and it was expected to do so.

All this is strong positive indication in favour of the independency of churches.

But to this we may now add the fact that, as we read the New Testament and observe the young churches in action, we also find strong negative indications against a centrally controlled structure. Certain elements essential to such a structure are missing from New Testament church life.

No church was given control over any other church and, conversely, no church is seen as under the control of another. Even the church at Jerusalem, though it was the first to be established and had a number of apostles within its ranks, did not claim the right to subordinate other churches to its rule. No New Testament church had authority over any other church, none gave orders to another, nor was any church regarded as superior to another.

No office was established for the ongoing life of the church that gave any official power to rule over more than one church. The apostles had such power, of course, but they were unique as eye-witnesses to the resurrection of Christ and as part of the very foundation of the church of Christ. They were not for its ongoing life. Paul is quite emphatic about this when he declares that the church as God's household is 'built on the foundation of the apostles and prophets, with Christ Jesus himself as the chief cornerstone' (Eph 2:20). To argue for bishops, popes, or modern apostles from the model of the New Testament apostles is just not on. You don't keep on laying the foundation of a house any more than you keep on adjusting a cornerstone.

There was no office created to replace the apostles, and the offices of elder and deacon that were created are concerned with the ordering of the local church from within, not from outside.

No council was constituted with power to rule over a group of churches, whether in a locality, a nation or many nations. Those who maintain that the New Testament has a place for some form of central government over local churches always refer to the so-called Council of Jerusalem convened in Acts 15. But the Council of Jerusalem was not really a council at all! It was a meeting of the church at Jerusalem at which representatives of the church at Antioch were present. It is true that apostles attended the meeting and had a part in the discussion and decision-making, and that it was a gathering that made decisions affecting the life of many more than those two churches, and that it has affected the policy of the churches ever since. But it was in itself a case of an aggrieved church referring its complaint to the church from which the offence came. It is not a model of episcopal government, for the complaint was not taken to a bishop. Nor is it a model of presbyterian government, for no presbytery met to consider the matter. Rather, it is a model of how churches should deal with matters of dispute that arise between them: the offended party should go directly to the source of the problem so that it can be speedily dealt with there.

During the period of the New Testament no council with power over a group of churches was set up either at Jerusalem or anywhere else.

No grouping of churches was designated by the word 'church'. That word was used for the universal church, the whole body of Christ, and it was also used for local churches. But it was used in those two senses alone; it was never applied to an organised grouping of local churches. When the churches in a particular area were spoken of, they were referred to as just that: the churches in Asia, the churches in Galatia, the churches of Judea, the Macedonian churches (1 Cor 16:19; Gal 1:2; Gal 1:22; 2 Cor 8:1). There is surely significance in this. Though churches in an area might have freely acted together, they were never regarded as under the authority of a denomination. Nor were they ruled by a committee for their area.

The local churches in the New Testament were both responsible and free. Each was responsible to Christ, the head of the church, to live according to his word and directed by his Spirit. None was governed by an outside body or official. They were independent churches, free to order their own affairs.

But that does not mean that they lived in splendid isolation, caring for no one but themselves!

21

Chapter 4
One Body

Independent the New Testament churches may have been, but isolated never. Though separated by considerable distances, they related to each other in significant ways and so demonstrated that they were one in the body of Christ.

We have seen that churches in the New Testament were at liberty to take up matters of common concern with other churches. The Antioch church and the Jerusalem church sorted out a problem that arose between them. The other churches were informed of the outcome and that proved invaluable to all the churches.

ONE IN THE BODY
A few moments spent travelling the roads of the New Testament will remind us of how the churches mattered to each other.

They kept in touch with each other
Though travel was difficult and dangerous, the flow of communication between the early churches was remarkably good.

The churches took advantage of the apostles' letter-writing to convey greetings for the encouragement of other churches. The church at Corinth was greeted by the churches in the province of Asia and by the church that met in the house of Aquila and Priscilla (1 Cor 16:19–20). The church at Rome must have been encouraged by the assurance of the love of their fellow believers when they read of the greetings of all the churches of Christ (Rom 16:16). When Peter wrote to a number of scattered churches, his letter was used to convey greetings from one church to others (1 Pet 5:13).

Paul's letters often gave news of the church where he was to the church he was addressing. Each of the last chapters of 1 Corinthians, Philippians and Colossians, and of Romans especially, carries news items for the readers' interest and prayers. The churches knew about each other and cared for one another.

The messengers entrusted with carrying the letters were chosen as people whose coming would be of spiritual blessing to the churches. Paul actually refers to such men as representatives of the churches and an honour to Christ (2 Cor 8:23). Other Christians who travelled around or moved to a different area enhanced the churches' knowledge of each other and they were commended by their own church to the other churches which they visited or where they settled (Rom 16:1–2).

The flow of communication between churches meant that one church could prove to be a stimulus and an example to others. So Paul tells the church at Thessalonica that it became a model to all the believers in Macedonia and Achaia (1 Thess 1:7).

The New Testament churches had a genuine concern and love for their sister churches. For example, Paul commended the Thessalonians for their love of 'all the brothers throughout Macedonia' (1 Thess 4:9–10). Such a loving concern is what we would expect. To 'love our brothers' is a mark of the new birth and of true discipleship (1 Jn 3:14; Jn 13:35). Loving concern for other churches is simply a way of expressing loving concern for all Christians.

They benefited from preachers and teachers who had a ministry to the whole body

The churches shared in the ministry of the apostles. Paul tells us of his 'concern for all the churches', a burden he carried every day (2 Cor 11:28). He did not merely plant churches, he visited them and wrote to them. Nor did he confine such a ministry to churches that he had planted; he wrote to and visited the church in Rome, for example.

Such a ministry to the whole body was not exclusive to the apostles. Other preachers and teachers moved among the churches: people like Epaphroditus, Timothy, Silas, Apollos, Tychicus and Erastus. In 2 Corinthians 8:18–19 Paul speaks of sending an un-named brother 'who is praised by all the churches for his service to the gospel'. It is interesting to note that this unknown servant of Christ was 'chosen by the churches' to help Paul in collecting funds for the impoverished Jerusalem church. Spiritual gifts are not simply for use in the local congregation of which a Christian is a member. They may be given by God for the benefit of the wider body of Christ.

They shared the letters in our New Testament

Though Paul, for example, might write a letter to one particular local church, that letter would be passed around the churches and accepted by them all as Scripture. When he wrote to the church at Colossae he told them to pass his letter on to the church of the Laodiceans (Col 4:16). The letter to the Ephesians, though intended for the church at Ephesus, is generally thought to be a circular letter shared by a wider circle of churches. The first letter of Peter was a circular letter shared by the scattered churches in Asia Minor.

Peter makes a fascinating remark about the apostle Paul's letters: it is encouraging for us to know that even Peter found in them 'some things that are hard to understand'! But what interests us particularly is that Paul's letters were known by the churches to whom Peter was writing (2 Pet 3:15–16). Clearly the New Testament churches shared the benefit of the letters with their needed mix of doctrinal and ethical teaching.

Of course this common reliance on the Scriptures produced a uniformity of belief in the churches, and of standards too. There were rules to which all the churches submitted (1 Cor 7:17), practices that all the churches accepted (1 Cor 11:16).

They cared for those churches in special need
The most obvious example of such practical care is the support that other churches gave to the famine-stricken church at Jerusalem. When the church at Antioch heard of the emergency there, 'the disciples, each according to his ability, decided to provide help for the brothers living in Judea. This they did, sending their gift to the elders by Barnabas and Saul'(Acts 11:29–30). Paul gave instructions to the churches in Galatia and to the church in Corinth about a collection for God's people, obviously assuming that each church would feel its identity with every other part of the body of Christ and would respond to the needs of the other. He expresses the principle of loving mutual help between churches like this: 'At the present time your plenty will supply what they need, so that in turn their plenty will supply what you need' (2 Cor 8:14).

So, though the local churches in the New Testament were independent churches, they were by no means isolated or disconnected. They knew about each other, cared for one another, prayed for one another. They kept in touch with one another, shared those preachers and teachers who travelled among the churches, shared the New Testament letters, and helped and supported one another when the need arose.

Our quick tour of the New Testament has brought into focus the inter-relating of the early churches. Their co-operating and their caring for one another were visible to any observer. But what could be seen was the outworking in practice of a deeper reality; it was the expression of the invisible spiritual relationship which existed between the churches. They were one in Christ.

ONE IN CHRIST
The New Testament has a great deal to say about the unity of the church. It uses a rich variety of picture-words to describe the church, each of which portrays the oneness of Christ's people.

The church is one family
The members of the 'whole family in heaven and on earth' (Eph 3:15) recognise God as their Father and each other as brothers and sisters.

The church is one flock
Christ the good shepherd who gave his life for his sheep is their one shepherd (Jn 10:16). He has only one flock.

The church is one people, one nation
Believers in Christ are 'no longer foreigners and aliens, but fellow-citizens with God's people and members of God's household' (Eph 2:19). They are one people, one nation (1 Pet 2:9–10).

The church is one temple
She is the dwelling place of God himself and she is holy.
This one temple is built on the foundation of the apostles
and prophets and they in turn are built on the one chief
cornerstone which is Christ: 'In him the whole building
is joined together and rises to become a holy temple in
the Lord' (Eph 2:21). Every believer stands on the same
foundation and each believer has his place in the same
developing structure. 'In him you too are being built
together to become a dwelling in which God lives by his
Spirit' (Eph 2:22).

The church is Christ's one bride
'Christ loved the church and gave himself up for her to
make her holy, cleansing her by the washing with water
through the word, and to present her to himself as a
radiant church' (Eph 5:25 – 27). He loved his bride; he
purchased her at the great cost of sacrificing himself, and
he loves her still. Christ's undeserved love is the same
for every believer. We are all unworthy of such love and
yet we are all brought into the closest possible relationship
with Christ. One with Christ we are one with each other.

The church is one body
This is the picture that is used most often to describe
the church, and the analogy of the body carries the
message of the unity of the church very powerfully.
Ephesians 4:4 declares, 'There is one body.' Ephesians
1:22 – 23 says that God has appointed Christ 'to be head
over everything for the church, which is his body'.
Colossians 1:18 says it again: 'He is the head of the body,
the church.' Other passages develop the idea more fully:
'In Christ we who are many form one body, and each
member belongs to all the others' (Rom 12:5); 'The body
is a unit, though it is made up of many parts; and though

27

all its parts are many, they form one body. So it is with Christ. For we were all baptised by one Spirit into one body' (1 Cor 12:12-13).

Though it is so wonderful that it is difficult to take in, the teaching itself is clear: Christ is the head and all who are believers are brought into union with him; they share his life, are members of his body, and, because they are related to him, they are related to one another. Belonging to Christ, they belong to each other. Sharing his life, they are one in him.

These pictures of the church combine to display the unity of the church of the Lord Jesus Christ. This is one of the major teachings of the New Testament and it can best be summarised in terms of its three basic constituents: *life, truth* and *love*.

The unity of the church springs from the possession of the same spiritual life. All who are members of Christ's body share that life. When Paul exhorts the Ephesians to 'make every effort to keep the unity of the Spirit through the bond of peace' he reminds them of all the things they share that make them one. 'There is one body and one Spirit – just as you were called to one hope when you were called – one Lord, one faith, one baptism; one God and Father of all, who is over all and through all and in all' (Eph 4:3-6).

The one Spirit brings life to those who were dead in their sins and constitutes them as one living body. They receive one hope, they acknowledge Jesus Christ as their one Lord and confess their one faith in one baptism, all under the sovereign grace of the one God. It is this possession of the same spiritual life that makes believers one and creates the unity of the church. After all, true churches are companies of people who have been born again.

The unity of the church is based on the acceptance of the same saving truth. Paul enforces his appeal to Christians to keep the unity of the Spirit by reminding them that there is 'one faith' (Eph 4:5).

The gospel creates the church, and gospel truth forms the basis for the unity of the church. Churches are made up of people of different ages, backgrounds, intelligence, temperament, employment, outlook and so on. These differences would naturally tend to pull them apart, but a common acceptance of the gospel and a common experience of the power of its saving truth brings them together. It is faith in Christ and in his atoning work that has brought them into the church in the first place, and it is a growing knowledge of him that keeps them together as they develop in Christian maturity and grow towards 'unity in the faith and in the knowledge of the Son of God' (Eph 4:13).

The unity of the church is expressed by the showing of genuine Christian love. Our Lord prayed for his people 'that all of them may be one' (Jn 17:21). Clearly the unity for which he prayed is a unity that can be seen because it is 'to let the world know' (Jn 17:23). The Lord Jesus commanded his followers to 'love one another' and that love in action demonstrates the genuineness of our discipleship and the reality of our unity (Jn 13:34 – 35).

Paul paints a picture of that love in 1 Corinthians 13; and in Romans 14 and 15 he spells out what this love involves in a most practical way. His teaching may best be summed up in the exhortation 'Accept one another, then, just as Christ has accepted you, in order to bring praise to God' (Rom 15:7).

Christ loved his church and gave himself up for her. We must follow in his footsteps and love all whom he loves, accept all whom he accepts. When we hesitate we must remember that we belong to him and to his church only because he loved us. Genuine Christian love recognises all believers as brothers and sisters just because they are believers and for no additional reason.

We have been looking at the life of the early churches, and we have found certain principles that must be applied to the life of the church today. How do we put these principles into practice?

Chapter 5

Big Problems

We have not discovered a detailed blueprint, but our study of the New Testament has shown us a pattern of church relationships. The New Testament churches were free and responsible under Christ to govern themselves and to run their own affairs, and they had good relationships with other gospel churches.

If that was the pattern, we must surely try to follow it. But that is by no means as easy as it sounds, for the church scene today is far more complicated than in those early days. Churches are now separated from one another by denominational structures which have long traditions and command strong loyalties. That was not so in New Testament times. Sadly, it has to be said that error and unbelief are deeply entrenched in the major denominations and this creates another division between these evangelicals who are within and those who are outside such denominations. That was not a problem for the New Testament churches which, whatever their failings may have been, were all essentially evangelical in their doctrine. The complexity of the church scene means that there are many cross currents. It is not always easy to determine how to steer a straight course.

Back in 1922 some evangelical churches got together to work out a solution to this confused situation. They formed the Fellowship of Independent Evangelical Churches, an association of churches that are evangelical in doctrine and independent in structure. It was established to encourage the churches in their stand for the evangelical faith and to help them co-operate in those activities which it was agreed were better done by churches together than by churches separately.

These independent evangelicals faced three major problems. First, they saw that many evangelical churches were isolated from one another and they believed that to bring them closer together would prove to be for the encouragement of all. Secondly, they saw the damage being caused by the rising tide of liberalism and wanted to raise the flag of adherence to the reliability of the Bible and the truth of the gospel. Thirdly, they saw with sadness the divisions that often separate one evangelical church from another and longed for a clear testimony to the unity of all Christ's true people.

The plan was simple. It was for independent churches, still ordering their own affairs, to express the oneness of the common life they have in Christ; the common experience of his saving power. All the churches that came together were united in the firm belief that life and power were to be found in the gospel of God's grace, so each church that joined confessed its adherence to the fundamentals of the evangelical faith. Deploring the fact that churches often divide from other churches on issues that are not fundamental to the gospel, they united on the essentials of gospel truth and agreed to differ on other issues. Of course, each church was free to have its own convictions on matters like the place of elders, the form of baptism and the interpretation of the millennium. But to separate from other believers on such matters, while being at one on the gospel, was regarded as wrong.

Today, many years later, these principles are still valid. The gospel is still primary, and the unity of gospel churches still needs to be demonstrated. And the problems faced in the 1920s are still as acute as ever.

THE PROBLEM OF ISOLATIONISM

There are areas of the country where there are very few evangelical churches and a local church can at times feel very alone. If fellowship among the churches is to be more than words, then practical steps must be taken to make sure that no church, and no pastor, is left out in the cold. Geographical isolation is not, however, the main problem.

Some churches become isolated through bitter experience. They may have tried to show good fellowship towards other evangelical churches in their area but have somehow got hurt. Understandably they are cautious about getting too close again; once bitten, twice shy. In spite of their agreement on the gospel, evangelical churches differ considerably in emphasis and practice and this can cause strain in relationships between them. Churches that differ can only relate well if there is mutual recognition of each other's doctrinal positions and mutual respect for each other's worship, ministries and disciplines.

Some churches seem actually to prefer isolation. It is possible for a church to be very much aware of its position as a local church, but to lack awareness of its part in the universal church. There are churches that are parochially minded; their horizons are limited to the boundaries of their own activities and their prayers are almost exclusively that God would bless *them*. They show little or no interest in other gospel churches nearby. As to the cause of Christ throughout the country, they seem never to have thought of that.

For a church to choose to live in splendid isolation when there are other gospel churches around them may display an underlying spiritual pride. The apostle Paul condemned such a self-centred attitude in the church at Corinth with a touch of biting sarcasm: 'Did the word of God originate with you? Or are you the only people it has reached?' (1 Cor 14:36). Things are pretty serious when we think that our church is the only true church.

Large churches and small churches can both become isolationist. Large congregations may not feel the need of others; small churches may feel threatened by others. But the truth is that churches do need each other. There is no church so self-contained that it cannot benefit from others. And the church that is well-endowed with gifts must consider the needs of other churches as well as its own. God has put us where we are for the good of the whole cause of Christ on earth, not to build our own little empires.

THE PROBLEM OF ERROR WITHIN THE PROFESSING CHRISTIAN CHURCH

Indeed, false teachings are rife at the present time. Our problem is to determine how evangelicals should react to error that is tolerated in some sections of the professing church.

Throughout its long history, the church has had to contend with the errors that come from the Catholic, or sacramentalist, tradition. These are serious for they touch the very heart of the gospel. The doctrine of baptismal regeneration blinds countless thousands to the need of conversion to Christ and of a true new birth. The teaching of transubstantiation diverts people from looking to what Christ fully accomplished for sinners when he died for them on the cross. The additions to the gospel are contrary to the very central truth of the gospel – justification by faith in Christ alone.

Since the middle of the last century, churches have suffered untold damage from those within their ranks who deny that the Bible is the word of God, and the major denominations in the United Kingdom continue to be swept by the tide of liberal theology. In many churches the gospel is not preached; in others basic doctrines of the gospel are openly denied. It is a shameful thing that the substitutionary atonement accomplished by Christ on the cross is rejected; that his deity is denied, and that even the personality and the Fatherhood of God himself is a matter of debate. Liberal theology that casts doubt on the Bible goes hand in hand with a situational morality that dethrones the absolutes of God's law and decides matters of right and wrong subjectively.

The modern ecumenical movement, working internationally through the World Council of Churches and locally in the Churches Together process, actually adds to the confusion. It refuses to define either a Christian or a church in any adequate, biblical way. All who claim to be Christian are accepted as such with no real test of the orthodoxy of their beliefs or of the reality of their spiritual experience. People are assumed to be Christian if they have been baptised or if they are members of a church.

Error does not remain static – it progresses. In recent years, some church leaders have made no secret of the fact that they no longer believe that Christ is the only way to God.

It is to be regretted that in the face of such a complex of error and unbelief, evangelicals do not speak with one voice.

Some stay in their mixed denomination hoping to win it back to its previous orthodoxy. No doubt when a denomination begins to depart from the faith, the first duty is to work for reformation within; to do all in one's power to call the denomination back to the evangelical faith it once proclaimed. But what is one's duty when there is no hope of the reformation of the body?

Independent evangelicals believe that at some point separation from error is our unavoidable duty. Indeed, a large number of people who are now in independent churches were once members of one denomination or another but felt obliged to leave because of the departure of their denomination from the evangelical faith.

Two factors determine the point at which to leave a denomination becomes a duty: the commands of Scripture which tell us to separate from teachers of error, and the effects of remaining within a mixed body.

Strong words are employed in Scripture to describe those who question the uniqueness of the person of our Lord and the value of his work of atonement. Those who deny the Lord Jesus Christ as fully God and fully man are called 'antichrist'. John tells his readers 'Every spirit that acknowledges that Jesus Christ has come in the flesh is from God, but every spirit that does not acknowledge Jesus is not from God. This is the spirit of the antichrist' (1 Jn 4:2-3). Those who pervert the gospel of Christ, whose adding to the gospel takes away from the sufficiency of the finished work of Christ, are 'anathema'. Paul writes to the Galatians: 'If anybody is preaching to you a gospel other than what you accepted, let him be eternally condemned' (Gal 1:9). Antichrist, anathema: the Bible takes the teaching of fundamental error as a matter of the utmost seriousness (see also 1 Tim 6:3-5).

But the New Testament does not simply speak strong words. It gives specific instructions concerning what true believers are to do about teachers of such error. The church at Rome is told to keep away from those 'who cause divisions and put obstacles in your way that are contrary to the teaching you have learned' (Rom 16:17). The church at Ephesus is commended by Christ for having 'tested those who claim to be apostles but are not' (Rev 2:2). Titus is instructed how to deal with a person who creates division. From the context it is clear that Paul is referring to someone who is spreading false teaching: 'Warn a divisive person once, and then warn him a second time. After that, have nothing to do with him' (Tit 3:10). These instructions are applications of the principle laid down by Paul in 2 Corinthians 6:14–18 that light can have no fellowship with darkness.

It is John, the apostle of love, who gives the most specific instruction as to how to treat a false teacher: 'Anyone who runs ahead and does not continue in the teaching of Christ does not have God; whoever continues in the teaching has both the Father and the Son. If anyone comes to you and does not bring this teaching, do not take him into your house or welcome him. Anyone who welcomes him shares in his wicked work' (2 Jn:9–11). John leaves us in no doubt as to how we should deal with someone who teaches fundamental error.

It is the failure of the major church bodies to discipline teachers of error that raises the issue of the duty of separating from such bodies.

But there is another consideration too. What are the effects of true evangelicals coexisting with non-evangelicals in the same body? Some stay in a denomination, where the majority deny the gospel, for the highest of motives: they desire to make a stand for the gospel. But the effect is actually to cause confusion as to what the gospel really is. The impression is bound to be given that the evangelical view is only one among other legitimate views. For evangelicals to associate with liberals or sacramentalists in the same denomination, or on the same ecumenical platform, does seem to imply that their interpretation of the gospel is just as valid as ours. No true evangelical can be happy with that, for evangelicals believe that there is only one gospel and that all else is not gospel. This is no little matter; the truth that God has revealed and the eternal destiny of lost people are involved.

The evangelical scene in our country is becoming increasingly complex. In recent years many evangelicals in denominations that are mixed doctrinally have moved from their policy of seeking to bring their denomination back to an evangelical position and now advocate a comprehensive view of the church in which they are happy to live alongside liberals and sacramentalists and to work with them for unity. This change in policy creates great problems for independent evangelicals who believe that true unity can only exist on the basis of a common acceptance of the gospel. The sad result is further division within the evangelical ranks.

The Bible teaching on separation is not popular. Current opinion is against it and most people stay where they are. The result is that many evangelicals are actually more closely associated with people who deny the gospel than with those who believe it and with whom they are truly one.

The cause of the gospel would surely best be served by gospel churches working together, uncluttered by others who do not hold, or who strongly oppose, the very message of God's good news.

THE PROBLEM OF UNJUSTIFIABLE DIVISIONS

The Scriptures strongly commend separation from those who teach error, but equally they command the maintaining of unity among true Christians. Many divisions are contrary to the great emphasis in the Bible on the unity of the body of Christ. Pride of denomination and the sectarian spirit that lies behind it are utterly opposed to the ethos of the New Testament and its teaching that the church is one.

Believers sometimes erect barriers between one another that are quite unnecessary. The reason given may be a difference on a point of principle or of doctrine, but the real reason may be little more than a clash of personalities or an undue loyalty to a leader (1 Cor 1:10 – 13). Even if a matter of doctrine is involved it must not be simply assumed that division on that score is (as, for example, in the Calvinist-Arminian debate) always justified. Any doctrinal difference must be seen in the light of the great doctrine of the unity of the church.

All truth is important, but there are different degrees of importance. There are primary truths which are of the very essence of the gospel, and other truths are always secondary to those. The authority of elders is not as important as the deity of Christ. The quantity of water used in baptism is not as important as the salvation pictured by it. A view of the millennium can never be as important as the fact that Jesus is coming again.

Of course, churches are free to have convictions on such matters, but it can never be right for church to withhold all fellowship from church on such issues. To make fundamental what is secondary can never be justifiable, and to separate from fellow Christians unjustifiably is to be guilty of schism – the tearing apart of the body of Christ. Schism is sin.

One issue that, more than any other, creates tension between independent evangelical churches at the present time is the whole question of the 'charismatic divide'. We maintain that we must associate with those who hold to the gospel but differ from us on secondary issues. That is not too difficult to do if the secondary issue is simply something like the amount of water used in baptism or even the age when baptism is appropriate. After all, each independent church can decide the details of its own church practice in the light of its understanding of Scripture, and there are many things that churches can do together that have no bearing on the subject of baptism. But there are some secondary issues that are not so easy to cope with. Difference of view on things charismatic is certainly in that category.

How can Church A have a meaningful relationship with Church B which insists that certain forms of worship and the practice of certain gifts are essential to a healthy church life and worship when Church A considers these to be unhelpful or even unbiblical?

On the other hand, how can Church B join in meaningful worship with Church A which denies the very gifts that have made life and worship so real to them?

However much we, on either side, insist that speaking in tongues, words of prophecy, calls for healing and so on are not primary matters, they become decidedly primary when we meet together for worship! Similarly, hand-clapping and arm-waving are matters of indifference to all of us in theory; but not when we are forced to remain inactive or become active against our personal preference. These things *do* divide us and it is pointless to pretend otherwise.

As a matter of fact our attitude to charismatic gifts may govern not just the way we worship but the way we evangelise as well. For some, the necessity of a baptism in the Spirit, speaking in tongues and the offer of healing, are all part of a full gospel presentation; for others they are not. How can we get through these barriers and express our unity?

Here is a possible way forward. We could start with an honest, frank and unembarrassed recognition of our differences; indeed, nothing can be achieved without that. The respective leaders of neighbouring churches could come together to explore how much these differences do actually matter and how much they are bound to cause division. Such a discussion may prove that some churches have a reputation they do not deserve! There may be a greater meeting of minds and a greater possibility of joint activity than either side would have thought. Agreement by the leaders on what is and what is not acceptable to each other's congregation may open doors for fellowship and worship together, and, with wise and firm leadership, this can ensure that both congregations can enjoy meeting together in a relaxed and non-threatening way.

Of course, the divisions may prove to be too important for one side or the other to relinquish. This should be frankly and lovingly admitted and, even though their styles of worship preclude closer association, areas of common cause may be found in which the two churches can work together.

It has to be said that there can be no meaningful fellowship where one side views the other either as spiritually inferior or as a potential convert. Local Bible churches must learn to respect one another even in disagreement, and the enticing of members away from their own fellowship into 'the light' of ours must be actively discouraged by all church leaders. In any locality churches will always find their preferred levels of fellowship in worship and evangelism; the regular meeting of leaders across the divides will help to avoid bad relationships and misunderstandings between churches that, though differing considerably, are one on the gospel.

The charismatic issue is, to a greater or lesser degree, here to stay. Independent evangelical churches can lead the way in showing how the problem of relationship it raises can be handled by local churches. But to do that we may need to start talking with those whom, up until now, we have been content to shout at or ignore.

There can be no doubt that the gospel that unites all true Christians is much, much greater than the issues that sometimes divide us. While we cannot associate with those who cast doubt on the gospel, we should seek to associate as closely as possible with those who hold to the gospel. Bible churches should come together and stay together – and in God's goodness they will grow together.

Chapter 6

My Church

'Do you come here often?' You are enjoying a weekend break and visiting an evangelical church you've heard about but have not been to before. The person next to you shows all the signs of being a believer but it's left to you to make the opening move at the end of the service. 'Do you come here often?' is the best you can think of on the spur of the moment.

'Yes, every Sunday,' replies your somewhat reserved neighbour.

'You're a member of this church, then?' Putting two and two together, you make five!

'Well no, not actually a member.'

'How long have you been coming, then?' you ask, thinking they must have recently moved into the area.

'Let's think. I suppose it must be getting on for twenty years.'

'But why . . .?'

If you attend a rally of a political party, you will be surrounded by members of the party: signed-up members. But when you attend a service at an evangelical church it is likely that a fair proportion of the people, though regular in their attendance every Sunday, will not be signed-up members.

Of course there will be some non-Christians present;

43

we are happy to see them in church and we long for their conversion. There will be children as well. But in many congregations there are often as many as a quarter of the people who attend the services regularly who, though professing to be Christians, are not members of the church. In new pioneering causes it may be less than that: in longer established congregations the proportion may be even more. It is a strange thing, but there are many people who claim to be Christians, and show all the signs of being genuine believers, who are not members of any local church. For some reason they have never *joined*. Why does such a state of affairs exist?

WHY DO SOME CHRISTIANS NOT *JOIN* THE CHURCH?

Some Christians are put off by the church
As they look on from the outside they see inconsistencies in the lives of some of the members. They feel that there is a lack of love or of warmth or of zeal. Maybe they know of some unfortunate incident in the history of the church or perhaps a long time ago they suffered from some misunderstanding that involved them or a member of their family. Unfortunately such things are not easily forgotten and act like stumbling-blocks keeping people from joining the church or at least making membership not as attractive to them as it ought to be.

The fact that there are weaknesses such as these in church life is no good reason for not joining the church, any more than the fact that some marriages fail is no good reason for not getting married. Of course we should look for a good church, as good as we can find, where the members show warmth and zeal and godliness, and the preaching of the Bible is taken seriously. But we have to face the fact that there is no perfect church: no

Christian is perfect, so no group of Christians is perfect. To quote the proverbial saying, 'If you find the perfect church, don't join it because you will spoil it!'

Some Christians don't want to get too involved
They realise that there are commitments and responsibilities that go along with church membership and to avoid those responsibilities they choose to sit like spectators on the sidelines when they ought to be down on the field where the action is.

Not wanting to be too involved is characteristic of the world in which we live. Ours is an age that emphasises rights rather than duties; an age that is happy to take all the privileges it can and to avoid responsibilities. Christians are in danger of being affected by the spirit of our age. But if we are fully committed to Christ, this always involves commitment to his church – and that includes a local church.

Some Christians are afraid to join the church
They feel that they have not reached a high enough standard in their Christian life to be a church member. They fear that they are not good enough, or that they don't know enough, or even that they might fail and so disgrace the church in some way.

A fear like that is actually a healthy sign; it shows that the church concerned is holy and that the individual concerned is humble. Yet however weak or inadequate believers may feel themselves to be, the place for them is inside the church family – not outside. Inside the church they can be helped, sheltered, comforted, encouraged and strengthened in their Christian life. We were never meant to go it alone.

Some Christians are muddled in their thinking about church membership

They say that you can be a Christian without joining a church and draw from that the false conclusion that church membership is an option to be taken up if desired, not an obligation to be fulfilled. Such reasoning is quite common. A few get even more bogged down. They argue like this: many people think they are Christians because they are church members; we know that you are a Christian only if you are born again, so church membership is unnecessary. This view assumes that church membership and the new birth are mutually exclusive! Of course you can be a Christian without being a church member, and of course you need to be born again to be a Christian, but that is no reason for not being a member of a church.

You can be a Christian without being a church member just as you can have an elephant without a trunk. Both are odd! You can be human without using soap, but life is better with it than without it. Soap is not essential for life, but it is essential for keeping clean. Similarly church membership is not essential for salvation but it is essential for living the kind of life the New Testament expects of those who are saved. We are saved by Christ and his work on the cross alone – not by joining the church – but that does not mean that any believer has the right to opt out of their biblical duty to join a fellowship of believers.

This leads us to another reason why some Christians do not join a church.

Some Christians question whether church membership is biblical

They believe in the church and in its importance, but they say that a stated membership is not something about which Scripture speaks and so they question whether a list of members – a church register – is necessary. They say that if we can show them a verse in the Bible that says, 'You shall join the church,' then they will join, and they think they have a really strong case because everyone knows that there is no such verse!

Yet 'Join the church' is exactly what the whole of the New Testament says *without using those actual words!* It is clear that our Lord assumed that his followers would be members of local churches (see Mt 18:15 – 17). The apostles gathered their converts together in local churches. A glance through the Book of Acts will show that this was their invariable practice. The epistles in our New Testament show that the early believers were addressed, encouraged and warned not just as individuals but as members of churches. The last book of the Bible, the Revelation, reveals Christ as still concerned with the local churches in the cities of Ephesus, Smyrna, Pergamum, Thyatira, Sardis, Philadelphia and Laodicea. The ascended Lord knows believers, notes their works, commends their good and condemns their sin – all as church members.

There is no verse that says, 'join the church'; there does not need to be – it would be superfluous. The whole of the New Testament assumes that true believers will be members of churches.

The question may, however, be pressed. Is formal membership with its list of members really biblical and necessary? The answer to that must be 'yes' for at least three reasons that lie on the surface of the New Testament and are easy to see. They concern decision-making, pastoral care and church discipline.

The New Testament speaks of local churches making certain *decisions* and the whole body having some part in that decision-making process (for example, Acts

6:1–4). Obviously, it must be clear who is entitled to share in the decision-making and who is not.

The New Testament speaks of elders who *care* for the flock as shepherds (for example, Acts 20:28; Heb 13:17). Again it must be clear who is under their care and who is the responsibility of some other shepherd.

The New Testament speaks of the sad necessity at times of someone being excluded from the church (for example, Mt 18:15–17; 1 Cor 5:1–2). For that to be practical it must first be clear who is included. Indeed, for any degree of church *discipline* to operate it must be beyond doubt who is included in a particular local church and who is not. It is surely obvious that a list of members is essential to the daily life and working of a church.

Even when people see that church membership is biblical there is one other reason why they may do nothing about it.

Some Christians don't see the value of joining a church
Let's go back to that weekend away from home and the conversation at the end of the service. 'But why have you never joined the church?' you ask the person next to you who has attended for twenty years but never signed up.

'I don't really see the point of joining. What would I gain by becoming a member?' The voice sounds a little tense, a little defensive.

Maybe that reply is more reasonable than it sounds, for the benefits of church membership are not always easy to see. But that is actually due to the generosity of the church itself, not because of the lack of benefits.

Most evangelical churches offer the warmth of their fellowship to all who attend, not just to their members: they care for all. In most cases they even accept people at the Lord's table, provided of course that they are believers, whether they are members or not. In fact in many churches the only thing that a non-member is not able to do is vote at a business meeting! This is all due to the kindness of the church, but none of it is a justification for not becoming a member.

The fact is that there would be no church for anybody to attend if there was not a body of members committed to it in the first place. People who are glad that the church exists, and who value its worship, its ministry and its fellowship, should identify with it fully and throw themselves into its life. Only the Christian who would be happy to see the church and its work disappear has any real grounds for refusing to join the church!

THE PRIVILEGES OF CHURCH MEMBERSHIP

The greatest blessing of all is to be saved by God's amazing grace, but linked to that is the privilege of being a member of a Bible-centred, Bible-preaching church. When someone applies to become a member of a church they are making a declaration of their salvation. They are saying, 'I am a Christian and I want to identify myself with this group of Christians.' And when they are received into the church, the body is also making a declaration. It is saying, 'We recognise you as a Christian.' It is a great privilege to be welcomed by Christian brothers and sisters as a member of the family of God and week by week to be accepted and recognised as one of God's people. Sometimes we take it for granted but that should never be.

It is a privilege to be part of a living fellowship
The church is not just an institution – it is a living organism. It is a body which shares a common life in Christ, not just a club that has a common interest in religion. Each member is part of that body and needs

the other members just as arm and leg, head and foot, ear and eye are parts of our human body and need each other (1 Cor 12:14–20).

A congregation is not just a number of isolated units stacked conveniently in pews like knives and forks in a cutlery drawer – close but unrelated. It is a body of people spiritually alive in Christ and vitally related to each other. There is a warmth of kinship in the Christian family not to be found in any other society, simply because all other societies lack that one essential ingredient of oneness in Christ.

The church is a living body itself, and it is busy with living activities. The church *worships*, and worship is a living thing, for the worship of God involves our whole being; all our heart, soul, mind and strength. The church *prays*, and prayer is a living conversation with the living God. The church *evangelises*: people who have new life go to people who are still dead in their sins with the message of life. The church *cares*: encouraging, correcting, comforting.

It is good to be part of a living fellowship that worships God, prays to him, tells out the good news and really cares.

It is a privilege to be entitled to pastoral care
Not that all the care comes from one man or a small team of men. In a living fellowship the members care for one another. Indeed, the apostle Paul says that it is the law of Christ that we 'carry each other's burdens' (Gal 6:2). But in addition to that Christ has given 'pastors and teachers' who are specially equipped to care for the church (Eph 4:11).

It is interesting that in the Bible Christian ministers are described as shepherds (Acts 20:28; 1 Pet 5:2), for the Lord Jesus Christ himself is our shepherd (Jn 10:11,

14). Christ calls his sheep by name; he leads and feeds his sheep; he guards them from danger. And this he does partly through under-shepherds who care for the flock and who make his shepherding the model for the way they shepherd the flock.

Much of the pastor's shepherding is done through the preaching of the word of God. Regularly each Sunday our souls are fed, the paths of righteousness are mapped out for us, we are warned of dangers. Some of the shepherding is done when individual members ask for personal advice. Sometimes the pastor sees that one of the flock is in particular danger and intervenes to rescue him.

Life is hard, the world is hostile, temptation is strong and we are weak and sometimes wayward. Christians need the shepherding that only the Christian church can provide.

It is a privilege to hear the word of God preached
It is no accident that in evangelical church buildings the pulpit is the focal point, and it is no mere tradition that the preaching of the word of God should be given priority in our meetings. True evangelicals give prime time to preaching the Bible because of what they believe the Bible to be.

We believe that the Bible is God's word, that all of it is God-breathed, and that it is the authoritative voice on everything that Christians should believe and on how Christians should act (2 Tim 3:16–17).

It is what the Bible is that forces the preaching of the word into the central place in the life of a true local church. Indeed, since way back at the time of the Reformation it has been recognised that the first hallmark of a true church is that it is a company of believers where the word of God is purely preached.

Times of revival have almost always been times of powerful preaching.

Immense benefits come to believers from a faithful preaching ministry. God speaks through preaching where the exposition of the passage of Scripture is true to the text, and the application of the eternal word is relevant, practical and heart-warming.

It does Christians good to hear a sermon on justification by faith, or on the loveliness of Christ, or on the power of his atoning blood, or on the Christian's pilgrimage, or on the city to which we are travelling.

People who believe that God has spoken in his word, and that God still speaks through his word preached, will not want to miss the preaching services of the church.

It is a privilege to share in the observance of the sacraments
It is a joy to be present when someone is baptised in the name of the Father, the Son and the Holy Spirit. It is good to gather with the family of the church around the Lord's table to do what Jesus told his disciples to do – eat bread and drink wine in remembrance of him. The Lord's Supper is a means of grace that we cannot do without; nor must we rob Christ of the devotion and love that can best be expressed in the communion service.

It is a privilege to be involved in the ongoing business of the church
A member of a church is entitled to attend church business meetings, to take part in the discussion and to share in the decisions that are made.

Humdrum, mundane . . . some items on the agenda may not seem to be very spiritual. But practical arrangements are necessary if the spiritual ministries are to prosper. The upkeep of the building, its decoration, heating and lighting and the cost of it all, may seem of little consequence in themselves, but these things must be attended to if people are to meet in comfort and to worship without unnecessary distraction.

Many of the items on the agenda will be of more evident importance: applications for membership, appointment of leaders, the call of a minister, plans for outreach locally, nationally and internationally.

Sometimes it is at the business meeting that the devil is the most active in disrupting the harmony of a church. It is a sad reflection on Christians that the atmosphere of the business meeting can be so radically different from the atmosphere of the prayer meeting. If church members were to realise what a tremendous privilege it is to have some part in the running of the affairs of the church of the Lord Jesus Christ, they would guard their words, put the good of the whole body first and seek above everything else that God's will be done in their church. God often makes his will for a local church known through a unity of mind and spirit that comes about during the discussion at the church business meeting.

There is always the other side of the coin. Being a member of a church lays on us considerable responsibilities.

If we were to make a list of the duties of church members it would include attending the meetings of the church (Heb 10:25), serving the other members of the church (1 Thess 5:11, 14; 1 Pet 4:8–10), obeying the leaders of the church (Heb 13:17; 1 Thess 5:12–13), supporting the funds of the church (2 Cor 9:6–8) and maintaining the unity of the church (Eph 4:3). These are all obvious responsibilities of church members and they are all important. Above everything else we must pray for God's blessing on the church.

The church is unlike any other society in that it is a spiritual body. Other societies emerge and grow by the natural laws of enterprise, hard work, social dynamics and man-management. While those laws affect the life of the local church to some extent, its life and growth depend on something else – Someone else.

When all is said and done, a church can only grow and thrive if it has spiritual life and power, and that can only come from God. For the church to be truly the church it needs the life of God; the breath of the Spirit. We must constantly ask God to grant that to our church and to all Bible churches.